CARING

with Bert and Ernie

A Book about Empathy

Marie-Therese Miller

Lerner Publications ◆ Minneapolis

Sesame Street's mission has always been about teaching kids much more than simply the ABCs and 123s. This series of books about nurturing the positive character traits of generosity, respect, empathy, positive thinking, resilience, and persistence will help children grow into the best versions of themselves. So come along with your funny, furry friends from Sesame Street as they learn about making themselves—and the world—smarter, stronger, and kinder.

—Sincerely, the Editors at Sesame Street

TABLE OF CONTENTS

What Is Empathy?

I care about how my ol' buddy Bert feels.

Empathy means you understand how someone feels.

A friend stays home sick from school.

You might send her a get-well-soon card.

I give Snuffy tissues when he has a cold.

How Feelings Look

People often show how
they feel with their faces.

When I'm happy, I have one big smile on my face.

Sometimes people show how they feel with actions.

How can you tell what another person is feeling?

People might stomp their feet if they are angry.

People cry when they are sad.

What might you do if your friend feels sad?

You can sit with them and listen.

13

You can share others' good feelings too.

When Elmo is happy, I feel happy too. We have a giggle-tastic time!

You might jump up and down with an excited friend.

People feel tired sometimes.
They might be cranky.

I tell fairy tales to Curly Bear when she is sleepy.

You understand they need rest.

Loud noises can be overwhelming.
Sometimes people need quiet time.

Empathy helps you understand how others feel. It connects people together.

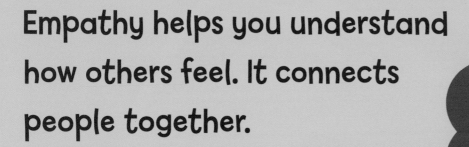

When have you felt empathy for someone else? What did you say or do?

BE A BUDDY!

Have your friends make believe they are feeling a certain emotion. For example, they might pretend to be sad, happy, embarrassed, or scared. Guess what they are feeling. What could you do to help them?

Glossary

connect: to join with others

excited: feeling very happy and eager

overwhelming: difficult or a lot

together: with other people

understand: to know

Learn More

Miller, Marie-Therese. *Me Love to Share with Cookie Monster: A Book about Generosity.* Minneapolis: Lerner Publications, 2021.

Murray, Julie. *Empathy.* Minneapolis: Abdo, 2020.

Nelson, Penelope S. *Having Empathy.* Minneapolis: Jump!, 2020.

Index

Photo Acknowledgments

Additional image credits: karelnoppe/Shutterstock.com, p. 4; anek.soowannaphoom/Shutterstock.com, p. 5; PR Image Factory/Shutterstock.com, p. 6; Rawpixel.com/Shutterstock.com, pp. 8, 19; Alena Ozerova/Shutterstock.com, p. 9; fizkes/Shutterstock.com, p. 10; jo.pix/Shutterstock.com, p. 11; Aynur_sib/Shutterstock.com, p. 12; Lopolo/Shutterstock.com, p. 13; Monkey Business Images/Shutterstock.com, p. 14; Liderina/Shutterstock.com, p. 15; kornnphoto/Shutterstock.com, p. 16; szefei/Shutterstock.com, p. 17; GOLFX/Shutterstock.com, p. 18; Robert Kneschke/Shutterstock.com, p. 20.

In memory of my son-in-law, Sean, who put empathy into action

Lerner Publications Company
An imprint of Lerner Publishing Group, Inc.
241 First Avenue North
Minneapolis, MN 55401 USA

For reading levels and more information, look up this title at www.lernerbooks.com.

Main body text set in Billy Infant. Typeface provided by SparkyType.

Editor: Rebecca Higgins **Photo Editor:** Brianna Kaiser

Library of Congress Cataloging-in-Publication Data

Names: Miller, Marie-Therese, author.
Title: Caring with Bert and Ernie: a book about empathy / Marie-Therese Miller.
Description: Minneapolis, MN : Lerner Publications, [2021] | Series: Sesame street ® character guides | Includes bibliographical references and index. | Audience: Ages 4-8 | Audience: Grades K-1 | Summary: "Bert and Ernie help young readers explore empathy. Kids will learn how to think about others, show that they care, and help those around them"— Provided by publisher.
Identifiers: LCCN 2020006278 (print) | LCCN 2020006279 (ebook) | ISBN 9781728403915 (Library Binding) | ISBN 9781728418704 (ebook)
Subjects: LCSH: Empathy—Juvenile literature. | Bert (Fictitious character : Henson) | Ernie (Fictitious character : Henson)
Classification: LCC BF575.E55 M55 2021 (print) | LCC BF575.E55 (ebook) | DDC 177/.7—dc23

LC record available at https://lccn.loc.gov/2020006278
LC ebook record available at https://lccn.loc.gov/2020006279

Manufactured in the United States of America
1-48391-48905-5/29/2020